Endc

It has been said that books don't change people, but trying to put into practice this one has changed me and my attitudes toward spirituality. The simplicity of the message has challenged my complicated understanding of my higher power... for the better.

– Mark S. host of The Recovered Cast Podcast
www.RecoveredCast.com

An ancient text, translated into current day, with easy to comprehend ideas. This is a true gift to modern day seekers of higher truth.

– Arlina Allen host of the One Day At A Time Podcast
www.OdattChat.com

After 30 plus years of recovery/sobriety, I feel I am still dipping my toes into the Fourth Dimension. Buddy C.'s interpretation of the Tao Te Ching has enabled me to open up another part of my spiritual heart that I did not even know existed. Who would have known a deep south southerner like Buddy could make the Tao Te Ching so interesting and compelling?

I am reluctant to use words like "inspiring" because words like that can seem overdone but... you can mark this book down as Inspirational. I would recommend this book to anyone seeking a deeper and more meaningful walk with the God of their understanding.

– John M. host of the Sober Speak Podcast
www.SoberSpeak.com

If you're seeking that "inner voice" and a clear path to know it better, let yourself contemplate, meditate, and celebrate it with *"Powerless but NOT Helpless."*

— Carl D. cohost of the Sober Pod Recovery Podcast
www.SoberPod.com

Powerless but NOT Helpless is an incredibly useful and instructive distillation of the underlying principle in each verse of the Tao Te Ching for those contemplating, or already living a sober lifestyle. Buddy proceeds to artfully combine this with a useful and direct correlation of each of these principles to universal tenets of 12-Step Recovery, further crystallizing the clear connection between them. The result is an indispensable resource for integrating Taoism into your regular recovery and spiritual practices.

— Charlie LeVoir host & producer of The Way Out Podcast
www.WayOutCast.com

This book is what happens if you put Lao Tzu, Bill W. and Buddy C. in a blender. Buddy has filtered each verse of the Tao Te Ching through a recovery lens. The result has great depth despite the brevity. I added spot illustrations that, I hope, slow the reader down, giving a place to pause and reflect.

— Don M. cohost of the Boiled Owl Recovery Podcast
www.BoiledOwlAA.org

Buddy's verses combine the timeless wisdom of Taoism and modern approaches to sobriety, guiding us to a fresh, yet familiar, connection with a Higher Power. Essential for anyone seeking a source of hope, joy, and peace of mind in their recovery program.

— Gigi Langer PhD, author of 50 Ways to Worry Less Now
www.GigiLanger.com

Buddy C.'s reinterpretation of the *Tao Te Ching* is a powerful meditation on the idea of surrender. His writing points to the mysterious, ineffable paradoxical power that makes both *The Big Book* and the *Tao Te Ching* effective road maps for finding, and staying on, "The Way." It's written with love and is a great guide for those looking to understand their Higher Power.

— Tod Perry host of the What's This Tao All About? Podcast www.WhatsThisTao.com

Buddy C. has a way of giving practical instruction along with describing the great paradoxes of recovery that is wonderful. Each passage should be carefully considered. I believe that study and meditation of these verses will help the truths contained in this book embed themselves in your heart. Although inspired mainly by the *Tao Te Ching*, I believe these interpretations stand on their own merit as highly useful and profound teachings.

— Jason Rudeen cohost of The Way Out Podcast www.WayOutCast.com

Buddy's interpretation of the Tao Te Ching helped me to bridge the gap between what I was taught about a Higher Power and how a Higher Power really works in my life. A resource I plan to use on a daily basis!

— Shane Ramer host of That Sober Guy Podcast www.ThatSoberGuy.com

POWERLESS BUT NOT HELPLESS

A Meditation Book of 81 verses from the Tao Te Ching that can help you live an alcohol free life and find freedom from any addictive behavior!

BUDDY C.

Edited by
KATE A.

Illustrated by
DON M.

Te Publishing

Copyright © 2021 Buddy C. and Te Publishing, Publishers

1st Edition, 2021

Paperback ISBN: 978-1-956024-00-5
eBook ISBN: 978-1-956024-01-2

All rights reserved, including the right to reproduce this book, artwork, or portions thereof in any form whatsoever. For information, contact the publisher.

Te Publishing
25 Liberty Drive
Unit 545
Cartersville, Ga. 30120-2206
info@TePublishing.com

www.BuddyC.org

The excerpts from Alcoholics Anonymous, the Big Book are reprinted with permission of A.A. World Services, Inc. ("A.A.W.S."). Permission to reprint these excerpts does not mean that A.A.W.S. has reviewed or approved the contents of this publication, or that A.A.W.S. necessarily agrees with the views expressed herein. A.A. is a program of recovery from alcoholism only - use of these excerpts in connection with programs and activities which are patterned after A.A., but which address other problems, or in any other non-A.A. context, does not imply otherwise.

The Twelve Steps of Alcoholics Anonymous have been reprinted and adapted with the permission of Alcoholics Anonymous World Services, Inc. ("A.A.W.S."). Permission to reprint and adapt the Twelve Steps does not mean that A.A.W.S. has reviewed or approved the contents of this publication, or that A.A.W.S. necessarily agrees with the views expressed herein. A.A. is a program of recovery from alcoholism only - use of A.A.'s Steps or an adapted version in connection with programs and activities which are patterned after A.A., but which address other problems, or use in any other non-A.A. context, does not imply otherwise.

Contents

Foreword   xi
Preface   xii

VERSE 1 ~ I ALREADY POSSES RECOVERY	1
VERSE 2 ~ OUR PAST IS AN ASSET	2
VERSE 3 ~ LIVING BY EXAMPLE	3
VERSE 4 ~ SOBRIETY IS INEXHAUSTIBLE	4
VERSE 5 ~ SOBRIETY IS FOR ANYONE	5
VERSE 6 ~ BE OPEN TO GOD'S GIVING	6
VERSE 7 ~ LIVING TO GIVE	7
VERSE 8 ~ THE NEXT RIGHT ACTION	8
VERSE 9 ~ PEOPLE PLEASING	9
VERSE 10 ~ SURRENDERING EXPECTATIONS	10
VERSE 11 ~ EMPTINESS	11
VERSE 12 ~ TURN THE LIGHT AROUND	12
VERSE 13 ~ WE CAN ESCAPE SUFFERING	13
VERSE 14 ~ THE WAY OF SOBRIETY	14
VERSE 15 ~ LIVING WITH EASE AND ACCEPTANCE	15
VERSE 16 ~ ALL TWELVE STEPS AS SEEN IN THE TAO TE CHING	16
VERSE 17 ~ THE PROGRESSION OF ALCOHOL	17
VERSE 18 ~ LIVING FROM THE HEART	18
VERSE 19 ~ THE WAYS I TRIED TO GET SOBER	19
VERSE 20 ~ I FEEL DIFFERENT	20
VERSE 21 ~ THE ELUSIVE PATH	21
VERSE 22 ~ YIELD AND OVERCOME	22
VERSE 23 ~ LIVING WITHOUT FEAR	23
VERSE 24 ~ ACCEPTING COMPLIMENTS	24
VERSE 25 ~ LOVE	25
VERSE 26 ~ HOW TO LIVE UNDISTURBED	26
VERSE 27 ~ EVERYONE IS MY TEACHER	27

VERSE 28 ~ BECOME THE CHANNEL	28
VERSE 29 ~ FORCE DOES NOT WORK	29
VERSE 30 ~ LIVING ABOVE THE PENDULUM	30
VERSE 31 ~ SURRENDERING THE WEAPONS OF FEAR	31
VERSE 32 ~ BE LIKE WATER	32
VERSE 33 ~ MASTERING YOURSELF	33
VERSE 34 ~ OUR LOVE NATURE	34
VERSE 35 ~ THE LIMITLESSNESS OF RECOVERY	35
VERSE 36 ~ THE MYSTERY OF SURRENDER	36
VERSE 37 ~ FREEDOM FROM ME	37
VERSE 38 ~ IMPORTANCE OF SPIRITUAL FITNESS	38
VERSE 39 ~ FINDING YOUR PLACE	39
VERSE 40 ~ LOVE IS THE BRIDGE	40
VERSE 41 ~ HOW TO SURRENDER	41
VERSE 42 ~ MY LOSS IS MY GAIN	42
VERSE 43 ~ THE VALUE OF SELFLESS ACTION	43
VERSE 44 ~ A CONTENTED MAN	44
VERSE 45 ~ STILLNESS	45
VERSE 46 ~ HOW TO FIND CONTENTMENT	46
VERSE 47 ~ I ALREADY POSSESS EVERYTHING	47
VERSE 48 ~ KNOWLEDGE AND SURRENDER	48
VERSE 49 ~ INNER DEPENDENCE	49
VERSE 50 ~ DYING TO LIVE	50
VERSE 51 ~ LIFE-GIVING LOVE	51
VERSE 52 ~ FOLLOWING THE INNER LIGHT	52
VERSE 53 ~ MY ONE FEAR	53
VERSE 54 ~ PRACTICING SOBRIETY IN ALL OUR AFFAIRS	54
VERSE 55 ~ A LOVING HEART IS YOUR STRENGTH	55
VERSE 56 ~ THE MYSTICAL UNITY	56
VERSE 57 ~ THE WAY OF PEACE	57
VERSE 58 ~ GOOD OR BAD	58
VERSE 59 ~ THE LIMITLESSNESS OF A SURRENDERED LIFE	59
VERSE 60 ~ PURSUE LOVE	60

VERSE 61 ~ HUMILITY IS THE KEY	61
VERSE 62 ~ OUR RECOVERY IS IN OUR EXPERIENCE	62
VERSE 63 ~ PROTECT YOUR PEACE	63
VERSE 64 ~ EXPECTATIONS	64
VERSE 65 ~ FREEDOM FROM KNOWING	65
VERSE 66 ~ WATER IS OUR EXAMPLE	66
VERSE 67 ~ THE THREE TREASURES	67
VERSE 68 ~ ANGER	68
VERSE 69 ~ HOW TO WIN THE INNER BATTLE	69
VERSE 70 ~ VALUE THE VALUELESS	70
VERSE 71 ~ SICK OF BEING SICK	71
VERSE 72 ~ THE SOLUTION BECOMES OBVIOUS	72
VERSE 73 ~ ALL IS AS IT SHOULD BE	73
VERSE 74 ~ THE CYCLE OF LIFE	74
VERSE 75 ~ STOP INTERFERING	75
VERSE 76 ~ SURRENDER TO WIN	76
VERSE 77 ~ HOW TO LOVE YOURSELF	77
VERSE 78 ~ EXERTING POWERLESSNESS	78
VERSE 79 ~ LOVE FORGIVES	79
VERSE 80 ~ TRUE CONTENTMENT	80
VERSE 81 ~ LEARNING TO LOVE	81
APPENDIX A: MORE ABOUT THE TAO	82
APPENDIX B: THE TWELVE STEPS OF ALCOHOLICS ANONYMOUS	84
APPENDIX C: MY INTERPRETATION OF THE TWELVE STEPS	85
APPENDIX D: SUBSTITUTING LOVE FOR GOD IN THE TWELVE STEPS	87
APPENDIX E: SUBSTITUTING EMPTINESS FOR GOD IN THE TWELVE STEPS (TAOIST VERSION)	88
APPENDIX F: SUBSTITUTING SURRENDER FOR GOD IN THE TWELVE STEPS	89
APPENDIX G: SUBSTITUTING TRUTH FOR GOD IN THE 12 STEPS	90
APPENDIX H: SUBSTITUTING GOOD FOR GOD IN THE 12 STEPS	91

APPENDIX I: VARIOUS VERSIONS OF THE SERENITY PRAYER	92
Traditional Short Version of the Serenity Prayer	92
Love Version of the Serenity Prayer	92
Empty (Taoist) Version of the Serenity Prayer	92
Surrender Version of the Serenity Prayer	92
Truth Version of the Serenity Prayer	93
Good Version of the Serenity Prayer	93
APPENDIX J: BIBLIOGRAPHY	94
INDEX	95
A PLACE FOR NOTES	105
A PLACE FOR NOTES	106
About the Author	107

Foreword

Powerless but NOT Helpless:
Written by Buddy C.

The Chinese spiritual classic known as the *Tao Te Ching*, or classic of the way and virtue, was formulated over 2500 years ago by the legendary Taoist sage, Lao Tzu. It has become the second most widely translated book in the world after the Holy Bible. In addition, it has stimulated innumerable applications and interpretations as divergent as the Tao of Physics to the Tao of Pooh!

However, one of the more innovative, practical and inspiring versions is this application to the recovery process by Buddy C., himself a recovery success. Entitled *Powerless but NOT Helpless*, this captivating book teaches how to apply the spiritual lessons of the ancients to the daily recovery challenges inherent with persons struggling with an addiction. Over and over, the ancient wisdom is applied to the tasks of self-love, learning to let go and surrender, and allowing natural wisdom to replace the inadequate lure of addictions with the path of wholeness that leads towards and is sustained by sobriety and recovery.

This unique volume of practical wisdom and spiritual truths has the power to help save many lives. It deserves to be widely read and applied as a balm to our modern dilemma of addiction. It would be a thoughtful and supportive gift for anyone you know who is in the recovery process. Books that inspire us to become our better selves are worth much. As such, *Powerless but NOT Helpless* is priceless!

By Dr. Carl Totton, PsyD

Licensed Clinical Psychologist
Director of the Taoist Institute, Los Angeles, California
Co-host of the Audio podcast: *What's This Tao All About?*

www.whatsthistao.com
www.drcarltotton.com
www.taoistinstitute.com

Preface

Finding a "God of My Understanding"

In Twelve-step recovery, finding a "God of my understanding" who helps with our addiction can be challenging. The process of surrendering to a Power Greater than myself is difficult, at best, and impossible for some. In hindsight, I see a lack of surrender kept me in a cycle of relapse for over six years. My difficulty was how to move from a belief that *did not* relieve my alcoholism to actions that *did*.

My Christian upbringing had given me the impression God only performed for those who believed a particular way – and in my opinion, almost no one I met who was practicing recovery qualified. Despite the differences, when I asked God to help me stop drinking by applying the Twelve Steps of Alcoholics Anonymous, I eventually stayed sober.

Still, like so many in recovery, the traditional views of a Higher Power did not resonate. I felt something was lacking in my "conscious contact." I began to research Buddhism, other eastern religions, and agnostic Christian writings.

As I researched, I was unaware of a pattern I began to see throughout all the primary religious texts. These were the same principles I heard in recovery.

I began to see three primary objectives:

1. Surrender to a Power greater than myself.

2. Clean up past harms with others and myself, resolving further harms quickly.

3. Help others.

My Discovery of Taoism

As I researched different belief systems, I found this story of the Vinegar Tasters (based on the painting by the same name).

This painting describes a metaphorical meeting between Confucius, Buddha, and Lao Tzu. These are the three men credited for founding the three major belief systems in China: Confucianism, Buddhism, and Taoism, respectively.

The three men were tasting vinegar by dipping their fingers in a vat, which was common in China during this period. Each man's reaction demonstrated his philosophy of life.

Confucius spit out the vinegar. He asked, "Why would anyone taste something so vile?" Confucianism is comprised of rules of conduct to correct moral decay and degeneration. Much of China today still follows many of Confucius's teachings, similar to the Old Testament Book of Proverbs.

Buddha swallowed the vinegar and suffered through the taste. He stated life is full of suffering. Just as he suffered through the taste of the vinegar, we suffer through life due to our desires and attachments.

Lao Tzu tasted the vinegar and smiled. Lao Tzu smiled, not because the vinegar was pleasant, but because it tasted just as it should taste – acceptance! Lao Tzu accepted the vinegar for what it was, already perfect – not needing his approval, disapproval, or effort to correct or fix in any way.

This painting reminded me of the story, "Acceptance Was the Answer" in the book *Alcoholics Anonymous*. The more I read about Taoist philosophy, the more I saw the application of principles I had learned in recovery. I started seeing AA Slogans like "all is as it should be" and "let go and let God," demonstrated in numerous Taoist texts.

I knew I had found what I was looking for in Taoist philosophy. Taoism's primary text is the Tao Te Ching – Loosely translated as "the book of the Way of Virtue." The Tao Te Ching (pronounced Dow-De-Ching) is the second most published manuscript globally, second only to the Bible.

Through years of studying the Tao Te Ching, I have found a practical spirituality that has helped me apply the Twelve Steps to all areas of my life, especially surrendering more of my will and life's cares to a Power Greater than myself.

Recently, I felt inspired (no doubt, from my years of connecting with the Tao) to share my experience applying the Tao Te Ching to my life in recovery. This interpretation of the Tao Te Ching is the result.

Keep in mind this is not a translation of the Tao Te Ching – *only my interpretation* **through the lens of my experience.**

I hope these verses will help anyone struggling to find a "God of their own understanding" and enhance your ability to surrender to a Power Greater than yourself.

You can use these verses in your daily meditations or at any time you are looking for comfort, guidance, or inspiration. They work for me, and I hope they work for you too.

Buddy C.
Atlanta, Ga
March 2021

Please note: In the back of this book, I have included a section titled "More about the Tao" and other appendices, including my interpretation of the Twelve Steps, several alternative versions of both the Twelve steps and the serenity prayer, plus a bibliography with further study resources.

Verse 1

**I Already
Possess Recovery**

The recovery I can create
with my thinking is
not real recovery.

When I think I know,
I have already lost
the understanding.
When I let go of
the need to know,
It is possible
to see the solution.

When I am obsessed with
formulas and shortcuts,
I only see the problem.

It is my fixed
way of thinking
that keeps me trapped.

Addiction and recovery
are both found within.
I already possess both
and have everything
I will ever need.

Verse 2

Our Past is an Asset

When we judge a thought
as a sober thought,
we create a drunk thought.
When we judge a day
as a bad day,
we create a good day.

A thought is only a thought.
Filtering all thoughts through a screen
of surrender and non-judgment,
we create fewer extremes.

We accept life as an eternal harmony:
indiscretions of the present, and even the
past, become assets of unknown value.

Our new life is not of our making.
We take no credit for our sobriety.

We share gifts as they come.
We surrender gifts as they leave.

We do not accept recognition
for the good we accomplish.

This is why our gifts last forever.

Verse 3

Living by Example

We do not idolize those in
recovery who appear to
have it all together.

Nor do we brag of our
accomplishments,
spiritual or material.

We use our experience
to put others at ease.
We show, by example, how
our lives have improved.

In turn, those desiring sobriety
will choose a similar path,
just as they are being shown.

Everything falls into place
the more we practice
this way of life.

Verse 4

Sobriety is Inexhaustible

The gift of sobriety does
not appear to be a gift at
all - until we surrender.
Then, there is a strength
beyond comprehension.

There is no fear so intense that
sobriety cannot bring relief,
no relationship so twisted that
peace is not imaginable,
no noise of life so loud that
harmony is not possible.

The truth is paradoxical and
hidden in plain sight.

I do not know who created
the principles we use;
it appears they are a part of all
conceptions of a loving God.

Verse 5

**Sobriety is
for Anyone**

Our Higher Power
and creation
treat all equally.

Sobriety is available
for anyone who
will do the work.

The principles of
recovery seem
empty of power.

Yet, they never fail
to provide when we
learn to surrender.

Verse 6

**Be Open to
God's Giving**

The Spirit that fills
the world never dies.
She is known as
the Great Mother.

She gives birth
to all of creation.
She is ever-present.

She never fails to do
for us what we cannot
do for ourselves when
we learn to be open
to Her giving.

Verse 7

**Living
to Give**

The universe
is everlasting.
Why do heaven
and earth endure?

They do not live
for themselves.
That is the reason
they are everlasting.

Therefore, the sober one
thinks of their needs
last, yet finds their
needs met with no
self-effort on
their part.

Their effort is in
helping others;
in turn, they are
perfectly fulfilled.

Verse 8

The Next Right Action

Water is an excellent example of
how to take the next right action.

Water nourishes all without
struggle or discrimination.

Water flows without trying to the
lowest places, places rejected by man.

In spirituality, live satisfied, always
open to the spiritual depth within.
In relationships, be kind
without an ulterior motive.
In words, be truthful
without deceit.
In leadership, be fair
without injustice.
In work, do your best
without an agenda.

In all decisions, move in rhythm
with the moment, seeking a way to give
rather than a way to receive, and you
will know the next right action.

Verse 9

People Pleasing

A cup filled to the brim
is difficult to carry.

People pleasing always
leads to problems.

Success never brings the
expected satisfaction.

If you're too consumed
with gaining approval,
circumstances will appear
to make you look foolish.

To truly accomplish your goal,
complete your task and
step out of the way.

In letting go,
you make room
for the Tao to
use your efforts to
their fullest potential.

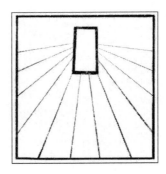

Verse 10

Surrendering Expectations

Can you ask your Higher Power to
take all actions necessary to bring
you to the point of surrender?

Can you allow yourself to come
to a place of full dependency,
like a newborn child?

Can you look within until your
reflection is Love and acceptance?
Can you practice Love toward
others with no manipulation?
Can you play the part assigned to
you in life without complaint?
Can you move from having,
to doing, to just being?

Living sober teaches us to Love
without a selfish agenda, to give without
expecting anything in return, and
to lead without dominating.

It is in the surrender of expectations
that we find acceptance.

This is called the highest of virtues.

Verse 11

Emptiness

It is the emptiness of the hub
that makes a wheel useful.

It is the empty space within the
cup that gives it purpose.

It is the space within the house
that makes the house livable.

The emptiness we allow
is our true value.

Verse 12

**Turn the
Light Around**

Data overload
can cause confusion.

Hearing too many loud
sounds can cause deafness.
Too many flavors can cause
the taste buds to dull.

Chasing excessive
wealth and fame only
confounds, never satisfies.
We only hinder our progress
if our quest is outward.

For this reason,
the sober one is
guided by their
intuitive inner voice.
They are not concerned
with the external.

They let go of
what is without.
Instead, surrendering
to what is within.

Verse 13

**We Can Escape
Suffering**

Glory or insignificance:
Which is better?

Both can bring suffering
when we are wrapped up
in self-will and ego.

As we surrender self
and allow powerlessness
to overtake our lives,
we will lose interest
in selfish pursuits.

We can then see how
to help those still
suffering, in turn,
escaping from
our suffering.

Verse 14

**The Way
of Sobriety**

Try to look, and
it cannot be seen.
Try to hear, and
it cannot be heard.
Try to grasp, and it
cannot be understood.

These three blend
together as one and are
beyond comprehension.

The aspects of sobriety that
are revealed are not dazzling.
The aspects of sobriety that
are hidden are not obscure.
Sobriety has no agenda, other
than to show you how to return
to your surrendered nature.

The Way of Sobriety
weaves through all of life.
What is this Way?

When I help you,
I am really helping me.

Verse 15

Living with Ease
and Acceptance

We do not have adequate words
to describe the Way of Sobriety.
We can only describe
its appearance.

The Way of Sobriety is subtle wisdom,
mysteriously powerful, and beyond knowing;
too profound to recognize with human intellect.

Cautious, like crossing a stream in winter.
Alert, as if surrounded by danger.
Courteous as an honored guest.
Relaxed as melting ice.

Unspoiled as a sculptor's uncut block.
Receptive as a valley awaiting needed rain.
Yet clear as a glass of pure water.

Who can be still, calm, and at ease until their
chaotic situation gradually becomes clear?

Like the settling of muddy water,
the right answer comes to life.

Verse 16

**All Twelve Steps as Seen
in the Tao Te Ching**

Our journey in sobriety begins with
Step 1: our introduction to emptiness.
Emptiness leads to the results of Step 2: peace and sanity.
Peace and sanity lead to Step 3: the flourishing of
our life, naturally surrendering to the Tao.

We become the witness to our lives in Steps 4 & 5: all of our past
brought into the light, given to our Higher Power, the source.
Steps 6 & 7 help us return to the root, bringing all of
our life in line with the never-ending cycle of the Tao.
We begin to see ourselves in our creator.
We begin to experience enlightenment.

We still have work to do in Steps 8 & 9. If we are not careful,
we will be reluctant to continue, and misery will follow.
Once we have completed Step 9, we begin to see even more
of the all-embracing, all-encompassing Love of God.

We continue the rest of our lives, living the union we have
found with surrender through Steps 10, 11, and 12. We move
from open-mindedness to acceptance to completeness to
Love and back again in a divine circle.

We are freed of fear and desire the more
of our lives we surrender.

Verse 17

**The Progression
of Alcohol**

The progression of alcohol
from a casual drink to
necessity can be subtle.

In the beginning,
alcohol is not noticed.
Next, alcohol is loved.
Then, alcohol is feared.
Eventually, alcohol
is despised.

Alcohol is believed
to have all control.

Only a gift as subtle as
sobriety can bring relief.

Like a child who receives
a gift, but plays with only
the box, we possessed
sobriety the entire time
and did not know it.

Verse 18

Living from the Heart

When the Way of Sobriety,
the Way of Love, is
abandoned in a life,
actions are no longer
from the heart.

We find ourselves helping others
because we are supposed to,
not because we want to.

We start wishing we no
longer have to be honest.

We pray less and attend fewer
meetings – we become agitated
at times for no apparent reason.

We eventually become a shell
of what we used to be, fear
growing behind every action.

If we do not
surrender again
to this Way of Love,
this Way of Sobriety,
we are destined to drink.

Verse 19

The Ways I Tried to Get Sober

All the ways I tried to quit drinking did not work.

Prayers were not answered; I prayed and
asked God for help, but no help came.
Self-knowledge was inadequate;
no matter how much I read
about alcohol destroying
my body, I could not stop.
Self-help was incomplete;
I could not try hard enough.
Getting sober for my family was also a
dead end. The threat of losing a job or
financial hardship could not motivate.
These were never sufficient.

I realized the solution through
surrendering to a Higher Power.
I lessened my selfishness and
fear through working the steps.
As I surrender to the rest of my life,
like I surrendered to alcohol,
I begin to experience the same
peace and relief in everything.

Little did I know my prayer had been
answered, but not in the way I expected.

Verse 20

I Feel Different

What is the difference between:
Yes and no? You and me?

The multitudes are enjoying the party.
I feel disconnected: Different

Like a baby that has not yet learned to smile.
I appear to be an aimless wanderer.
I, alone, seem left out.

Most people have a goal or a purpose.
I, alone, look to be drifting
with no clear objective.

Like a rudderless boat on the ocean,
blown by the wind.

I am different from the masses:
Why?

I am learning to live in the
moment and leave the outcome of
my actions to a Higher Power.

With time, the dis-connection becomes
connection on a deeper level.

Verse 21

The Elusive Path

As alcoholics, real life
comes when we follow
the Way of Sobriety.

What is this Way?

Utterly elusive
and intangible,
like the light of
the full moon.

Even though our
descriptions are vague,
we can see its fruit.

With gratitude, we can
look back through
our lives and see
evidence of this Way
at work in all things.

How do we know this?
By looking within.

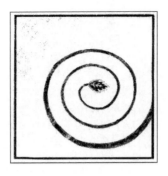

Verse 22

Yield and Overcome

You must first surrender to be made complete.
If you want to be vindicated, you must first be accused.
If you want to be filled, you must first be empty.
If you want to be healed, you must first be sick.
If you want to succeed, you must first fail.

Excessive desires cause one to lose
their way. The sage clings to Love. As a result,
she has the ability to discern the next right action.
She does not show off and is not focused
on herself, therefore she is clear-sighted.

She does not claim to be right or
wrong, therefore she flourishes.
She does not indulge in self-praise,
therefore she succeeds.
To the extent that she does not quarrel,
no one quarrels with her.

The ancient saying, "Yield and
overcome," is not just empty words.
This truly is the perfection
that comes from surrender.

All who make this practice a
way of life will be made complete.

Verse 23

Living Without Fear

Be like nature: accept
what is without fear.

A gale does not
last all morning;
it is only wind.
A cloudburst does
not last all day;
it is only rain.

Accept the actions of
others just as we accept
the actions of nature.

Practice the Way in all
your affairs; then you
can live without fear.

Do not fear success; then
you can thrive in success.
Do not fear failure; then
you can thrive in failure.

How is this possible?
By helping someone else
overcome their fear.

Verse 24

Accepting Compliments

One who tiptoes
does not stand firm.
One who straddles a
ditch cannot move fast.
One who shows off
is not walking
in the Way.

If you arrogantly insist
on being right, you will
always be wrong.
One who blinds others
with their success
will ultimately fail.

One who follows the Way
does not do these things.
They learn to look at their life
with gratitude and accept all
as a gift to be given away.

When complimented,
they can say "thank you"
but are really saying
"thank You" to a
Higher Power.

Verse 25

Love

There was "something" containing
everything before the world began.
Empty, complete, unchanging, tranquil,
formless, ever-giving, and in
constant motion, without effort.

This "something" permeates
everything, accessible everywhere.

If I were to impose a name, I would call
it the "Tao," the "Way," or "Higher Power."

This Way is functioning everywhere,
ever-flowing and always returning.

Man follows Earth, Earth follows the
Universe, the Universe follows the Way.
The Way always follows
its nature of Love.

These four are the great ones.
They naturally follow each other in
a continual, harmonious dance of Love.

On second thought, I think I will call
this "something" Love!

Verse 26

**How to Live
Undisturbed**

Compassion
makes life easy.

Surrender is the
master of the restless.

Therefore, those living
sober can participate
in the activities of the
world, undisturbed
and without fear.

They can enjoy many
material goods yet
stay unattached.

As long as compassion
and surrender continue,
all of this is possible.

Verse 27

**Everyone is
My Teacher**

Good works leave no trace.
Good plans use no schemes.

Those living sober rescue
others and reject no one.

This is called
following the light.

We learn from the most
unlikely teachers and influence
the most unlikely students.

If we are not
open-minded as to what
we can receive from others,
especially those who we feel
have nothing to teach us, we
will end up utterly lost.

This is essential wisdom.

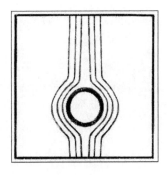

Verse 28

Become
the Channel

Practicing the principles
we learn in recovery
will bring us back
to the ease of
childlike dependency.

Know those who are
virtuous, but serve
the disgraceful
and shameful.

In doing so,
we can become
a channel of grace
for the sick and
suffering.

The more we surrender,
the more we transform,
and the more we
can be used.

Verse 29

Force Does Not Work

Can we improve our
world through force?
I do not think it can be done.

The world is beyond our ability to
change and may already be perfect.

If we try to force our will, we will fail.
There is a time to lead, a time to follow;
a time to feel relieved, a time to panic;
a time to grow, a time to decay;
a time to win, a time to lose.

Abandon sweeping
judgments and reject excess.
How is this possible?

By living in compassion,
we can view life as
a divine harmony,
beyond our control.

We can find
peace and acceptance
where others find
fear and angst.

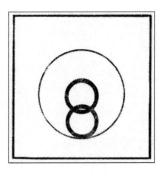

Verse 30

Living above the Pendulum

Force is like a pendulum. Every action
has an equal and opposite reaction.

One that is living in harmony with the
Way seeks to live above the pendulum.

How? By looking for opportunities
to help in daily life rather than
intimidate and dominate by force.

Similar to an encampment once an
army has left, after the use of force,
there are only briars and thorns
with famine soon to follow.

When we push, manipulate, and control,
we always meet a counterforce.

Regardless of whether we are
dealing with events, people,
thoughts, emotions, or
feelings, we cannot escape
the consequences of resistance.

This is not the Way. Anything not
of the Way will come to an end.

Verse 31

Surrendering the Weapons of Fear

The weapons of fear are
selfishness, dishonesty,
and resentment.

When we start this path,
these are the only
defenses we possess.

The result is weakness,
despair, and death.

As we surrender to this
new way of life, we begin
to lay down the weapons of
fear and pick up the gifts
of Love in their place.

We see our enemy
was not the target
of our fear.

There is no enemy,
only ourselves.

Verse 32

Be Like Water

The Way is like a rolling river;
constant, indefinable,
seemingly endless.

Its manifestations are subtle.
No one can tame it.

Surrendering to this flow
allows harmony, even in the
most difficult circumstances of life.

Beware of the trap of division.
Once we begin to label this as beneficial,
or that as harmful, we are headed for peril.

The Way is always present,
like streams running into rivers,
eventually leading to the ocean.

Water continues to flow, offering no
resistance, letting gravity do all the work.

Surrendering to the moment, we are to be
like water, doing the next right
action that appears in our path,
following this flow of Love.

Verse 33

Mastering Yourself

If you know others,
you have wisdom.
If you know yourself,
you are truly enlightened.

Mastering others
takes outward power.
Mastering yourself
takes inner surrender.

He who continues to
exert powerlessness
over himself and
others will succeed.

He who surrenders
to this life will
never taste death.

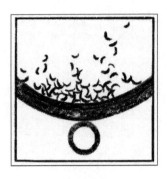

Verse 34

Our Love Nature

Love is all pervading,
expansive, like an ocean!
Love reaches in all
directions and touches
everything in the world.

Love gives life to all,
holding back nothing.
Love provides even for the
most seemingly insignificant.

Love does its work
and takes no credit.
Love feeds all without
lording over any.

Love, not being trapped
by desires, can fulfill
the needs of others.

The sage does not
wish to be great, so she
accomplishes great things.

I think I will surrender to my
nature of Love and enjoy!

Verse 35

**The Limitlessness
of Recovery**

Those who grasp Recovery
attract all good things,
enjoying peace and
contentment without
suffering harm.

Travelers who pass by
may stop if they hear
music or smell fine food.

Words spoken about
Recovery seem dull
and uninteresting.

Look, and there
is nothing to see.

Listen, and there
is nothing to hear.

Surrender, and
Recovery is
limitless!

Verse 36

The Mystery of Surrender

I must stop resisting
my addiction for
recovery to work.

To weaken something,
I must first stop
resisting its strength.
To reject something,
I must first accept it.

To possess something,
I must first give it away.

This is called the
mystery of surrender.

The submissive and
flexible overcome the
resistant and unyielding.

Unless I learn to
give when I am in need,
the application of this
truth remains hidden
in deep waters.

Verse 37

**Freedom
from Me**

The Way of Sobriety
never acts from
self-interest, so there
is nothing to correct.

When I abide in the Way,
everything marches
in a divine rhythm.

When old fears raise their
heads, surrender removes
any remaining power
they may have.

I am aware that all of
my character defects
have their origin in fear.

As I surrender to the fears
that bind me, I am freed
from myself and able to
be of service to others.

Verse 38

Importance of Spiritual Fitness

If we are spiritually fit, we are
not conscious of our Love nature.
Thus we begin to Love without trying.

When we try to Love through our own abilities, there is
always a fear to protect, so our attempts to Love are hollow.
Because we keep trying, we are never able to Love.

If we lose our spiritual fitness, we may
experience the following spiral downward:
The best we can do within our own
power is an empty kindness; the peace
we used to experience is no longer there.
Next is morality; we try to Love
because we are supposed to.
When the work is not complete, we
roll up our sleeves and force completion.
Next is ritual; only a shell remains of what was
once real. Finally, there is unmanageability.

Therefore, the spiritually fit
dwell in the fruit, not in the flower.
We discard what is outward, surrendering
to what we already have within. As a result,
our outward actions are not contrived
and become effortless works of Love.

Verse 39

Finding Your Place

At one with Love, sky is clear, earth is at
peace; man's soul is divinely inspired.

Without Love, sky is filthy, earth is
at war; man's soul is in turmoil.

Therefore, dependency is
the root of the Way.
Surrender is the foundation.
For this reason, sober ones refer
to themselves as powerless.

Carriage wheels are useless
without the rest of the carriage.
The hand is useless without
the rest of the body.

Unless we learn to let Love have
its way, we cannot be content.

If we jingle like jade or rumble like rocks,
we have to accept ourselves in the light
of Love, showing us our place in the body.

Then our purpose in life will
become apparent and satisfying.

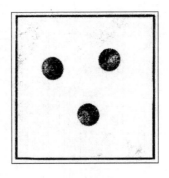

Verse 40

Love is
the Bridge

Love is a continuous cycle
of giving and receiving.

The Tao works through our
Love-motivated actions.

Starting from what is,
Love is the bridge
to what is hidden
in plain sight.

Verse 41

How to Surrender

The one genuinely seeking sobriety
surrenders with all their heart.
The one who thinks they are ready
surrenders until it is uncomfortable.
The fool laughs out loud and exclaims,
"it couldn't be this simple!"
If the fool did not think it ridiculous,
surrender would be useless.

The brightest way seems dim;
moving forward seems
to be withdrawing.
The straight seems crooked;
the smooth appears rough.
The prosperous seems destitute;
the innocent seems disgraced.
The all-inclusive path seems inadequate;
the genuine seems fraudulent.

The thread concealed in the fabric of
all things is available to the one
who knows how to surrender.

How do I surrender?
Let the God of my understanding know
I want to get sober, regardless of what it takes.

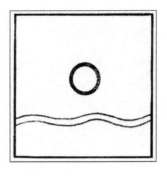

Verse 42

My Loss is
My Gain

The Tao gives birth to
the unity of all things.

This unity gives birth to the two;
The two give birth to the three;
The three give birth to all things.

All beings repeat this principle,
carrying the Yin and containing the Yan.
Combine these life forces to produce
the place of effortlessness.

No one wants to be orphaned, widowed,
or without food, yet noble rulers refer
to themselves by these labels.

Sometimes, in losing, we make
room for gain, and in gaining,
we make room for loss.

The question to ask may be,
"What can I lose today?"

I will make this the
basis of my teaching.

Verse 43

**The Value of
Selfless Action**

That which yields
overcomes the
hardest substances.

That which has
no resistance
finds room where
there is no space.

Therefore, know the
value of selfless action,
allowing personal
experience to
be your teacher.

The world seldom
comprehends
these principles.

Verse 44

A Contented Man

Fame or dishonor,
which is loved more?
Your life or wealth,
which is more valuable?

Gain or loss, which is
more distressing?
The stronger
the attachment,
the greater the loss.

A contented man
is immune to
disappointment.

If you know when
enough is enough,
you will be
free of trouble.

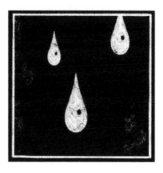

Verse 45

Stillness

Great achievements seem
lacking, yet their usefulness
is not exhausted.

Great abundance seems empty,
but its fullness never ends.

Great truth seems unjust.
Great intelligence seems clumsy.
Great eloquence stammers.

Motion overcomes cold.
Keeping still overcomes heat.

The order of the universe
can be observed in stillness.

Verse 46

How to Find Contentment

Those living sober use
their energy to help others.

Those not following this
Way use their energy
to control others.

There is no greater curse
than wishing you
were someone else.

There is no calamity greater
than hating yourself.

Therefore, the one that
is content will
always be enough.

How do we find
contentment?

By showing others
they are enough.

Verse 47

I Already Possess Everything

Perhaps —
There is no wisdom
one can discover
outwardly
that one does not
already possess within.

Verse 48

**Knowledge
and Surrender**

One seeking knowledge
learns something
new every day.

One seeking Sobriety
surrenders something
new every day.

Verse 49

**Inner
Dependence**

The Way of Sobriety
lessens self-interest.
This allows awareness
of the needs of others.

For example, those who
are good are treated as good.
Those who are not good are
treated with the same goodness.
Thus, inner goodness is attained.

Those who are loyal
are treated with devotion.
Those who are not loyal are
treated with the same devotion.
Thus, inner devotion is attained.

With time, this Way of Living will
bring our lives to a place of
inner dependence in all
things, much like a
child to a loving parent.

Verse 50

Dying to Live

All who have drawn
a breath abide in one
of these categories:

About a third live
cautious, uneventful lives.

About a third are
self-destructive, reckless,
and overindulgent.

About a third start out
living a full life, then
unknowingly, are
overtaken by fear.

A small fraction find
a way of living that
frees them from
the fear of death.

How is this possible?
They have already died.

Verse 51

Life-Giving Love

Sobriety gives life
to all who seek.
Love shapes and
gives form.
Circumstances
complete.

All honor this
Way of Love
spontaneously,
whether they
wish to or not.

It is the nature of all.

This Way gives all
but does not possess,
acts without expecting
gratitude, cultivates growth
without interfering.

How do we touch this
deep and profound Love?

We surrender to what is.

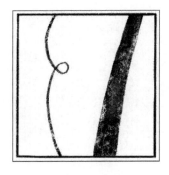

Verse 52

**Following the
Inner Light**

At the beginning of
our quest for Recovery
we begin to see what
our life can be.

We start experiencing
freedom from fear in
our everyday lives.

Learning to trust
this intuitive inner
voice is a yielding that
brings great strength.

Insight is restored
and we begin to
avoid misfortune.

This is called
returning to the
nature of one's origin.

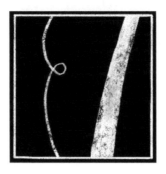

Verse 53

My One Fear

If I had a fear, it would be
straying from this Way.

This Way is broad and easy,
but I prefer to take side
roads and shortcuts.

I prefer to talk about
spiritual axioms
while I conceal anger
and resentment.

I like to sound spiritual
in meetings and
pretend I do not feel
I am better than others.

This behavior is far
from the Way and
always leads me
toward a drink.

Verse 54

Practicing Sobriety
in All Our Affairs

We are not easily shaken
if we are rooted in Sobriety.

If we follow Sobriety, we will
be honored for generations.

If we practice Sobriety
in our inner self, our
Love is genuine.

If we practice Sobriety
in our family, our Love
is more than enough.

If we practice Sobriety
in our business, our
Love is respected.

If we practice Sobriety
everywhere, our Love
is envied by all.

How do we know this?
By the cultivation
of Love within.

Verse 55

**A Loving Heart
Is Your Strength**

One who possesses Love
in abundance is like
a newborn child.

Poisonous insects will not sting.
Wild beasts will not attack.
Birds of prey will not strike.
Nature makes room
and does not harm.

His bones are flexible
yet he has a firm grip.
Nothing will be asked of him
that he is not able to accomplish.
He lacks understanding, yet is
perfect in all ways, needing nothing.
He can cry all day without
getting hoarse.

Harmony is at its height; there is no fear.
He is in the moment at all times.

Reacting out of fear can be disastrous.
A dependent, loving heart
is your strength.

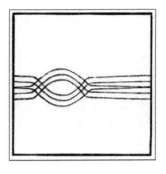

Verse 56

The Mystical Unity

The one who knows
how to Love does
not have to speak.

The one who is fearful
speaks continually.

Sit in silence
until sharpness
becomes dull.

Allow complexity in
personal relationships
to loosen without
your interference.

Let dust settle so
you can see clearly
what is already there.

Eventually, you will
realize you are me,
and I am you: the
mystical unity.

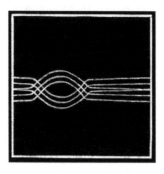

Verse 57

The Way of Peace

Let Love govern your decisions.
Let paradoxical truth make
your choices for you.
Become the observer
in your everyday life.

When you make fear-based
decisions rather than
Love-based decisions, the
result is always more fear.

The more you focus
on your defense, the
more you are attacked.

It is possible to allow your
day to evolve without
excessive effort or control.

How? By lessening desires
and letting go of expectations
of yourself and others.

You then find the simple
grooves of life that lead you
in the Way of Peace.

Verse 58

Good or Bad

Govern your life from a distance,
and you will be free of self-deceit.

Constantly meddle in your
affairs, and relieving misery
will become your motivation.

Disaster has its root in good fortune.
Happiness lurks beneath hardship.
Who knows what the future holds?
Is there right or wrong?

Good seems bad.
Bad seems good.

This has always been a mystery
and has led the most sincere
among us astray.

Therefore, the sage resists
judging her day and accepts
the moment for what it is.

She uses her brilliance not to blind,
but to show the Way to others
that she is already walking.

Verse 59

**The Limitlessness of
a Surrendered Life**

In daily life, there is nothing
better than surrender.

No one can perceive
the limits of a
surrendered life.

Surrender is the
foundation of
a life of Love.

Allowing Love to be
your guide, letting go
of what is, your entire
life can be transformed.

Verse 60

Pursue Love

Running our lives is
like cooking a small fish;
less is better.

We are not Godless
or evil, but fearful
and directionless.

What is the solution?

We ignore fear and
pursue Love.

With time, the fear we
see diminishes: a path
of Love becomes
uncomplicated
and effortless.

Verse 61

**Humility
is the Key**

The farther we progress
on this path, the more our
ego diminishes, like rivers
flowing to the ocean.

The greater the
body of water, the
more it continually
gives back to
the world.

Through experience,
we find the more humble
our walk, the more
grace we attract.

The more grace we
attract, the greater our
spiritual awareness.

The greater our spiritual
awareness, the more we
are able to give back
to those around us.

Verse 62

**Our Recovery Is
in Our Experience**

Anyone caught in the grip
of alcoholism desires relief.
Sobriety is their refuge.

Someone blinded
by fear is only able
to look outward in an
attempt to stop drinking.

Do we abandon such a person?
Never!

Do we shower them with help?
No!

Do we give them advice
as to how to stop drinking?
Absolutely Not!

The relief is in
sharing our experience:
how we stopped drinking!

This is the path to Sobriety
for anyone who will follow.

Verse 63

Protect Your Peace

Forsake self-serving actions.
Serve without expecting
anything in return.

Repay bitterness
with kindness.

Every offense starts
with a single act.
Fix relationships while
the offense is still small.

The sage never attempts to
accomplish great things.
Therefore, she is great.

She knows her peace
is in showing others
her path to peace.

Therefore, her peace
is protected.

Verse 64

Expectations

Anytime I manipulate,
trying to force a wanted result,
I defeat my own purpose.

Whatever I try to control
I will ultimately lose.

I can pursue success,
but it will remain
just out of reach.

Thus the sage accepts the
end result just as she
accepted the beginning.

Being free of desire, she
possesses genuine compassion
for the desires of others.

Her wisdom is in her experience,
not in her education or knowledge.

She allows everything to take its
natural course of action without
interference or expectations.

Verse 65

Freedom from Knowing

Freedom from ourselves
is the Way of Sobriety.

We can be no further
from the truth than
when we think we know.

Replacing our knowledge
with open-mindedness,
abandoning what we
think we know, being
open to learn from
the experience
of others:

This is hidden virtue.

Verse 66

Water is Our Example

Water flows downward.
This is why the larger the
body of water, the lower it is.
The larger the body of water,
the more it continuously gives
back through evaporation.

If you desire to be humble,
you must serve. If you want to live
carefree, take on the care of others.

If you want to be free of fear, pray for
someone else to abandon their fear.

If you want to be free of an addiction,
share with someone else how you are
surrendering to your addiction.
If you want to be successful,
help someone else succeed.

If you want to be Loved,
Love someone else.

If you stop competing and
serve instead, no one is able
to compete with you.

Verse 67

The Three Treasures

This Way of Surrender
has been around
since the beginning.

It is so simple most
overlook its strength.

I have three treasures
I guard with all my heart.

These three are:
the freedom to Love,
the freedom to give,
the freedom to be humble;
to perceive everything as
a gift to be given away.

These three work
together much like a
trinity of divine purpose.

All fight has disappeared.

No defense is necessary.

Verse 68

Anger

The greatest warrior
is not violent.

The most skillful fighter
in battle is not enraged.

The greatest champion does
not provoke his enemy.

The one that finds a way to
show compassion instead of
anger will be victorious.

Showing Love brightens your
hidden path to inner Love,
making anger insignificant.

In this Way, the negative actions
of others work to your benefit.

This is the Way of the ancients,
the Way of the Tao.

Verse 69

**How to Win
the Inner Battle**

The generals have a saying:
"It is never wise to
make the first move."

They would rather
withdraw a foot than
press forward an inch.

This means advancing
without appearing to do so.

There is nothing worse than
underestimating your enemy.

This also applies to the
inner enemies of selfishness,
dishonesty, resentment, and fear.

If you are not careful, you
can lose your three treasures.

Who wins the inner battle?

The one who knows
how to surrender.

Verse 70

Value the Valueless

My teachings are easy to
understand and very easy
to put into practice.
Yet few do.

My words have
an ancient beginning.

The affairs of man
are by design.

People are ignorant
of that design so they
do not follow my ways.

Turn the light around
and surrender your way
within, and you will reach
your inner treasure.

Therefore, the sage
values what appears to be
valueless, but in reality
is the most precious.

Verse 71

**Sick of
Being Sick**

Knowing we do not know
is the highest knowledge.

Thinking we know
is an illness.

We unlearn by working
through the pain of
living life our way.

The sage meets no difficulty
because he has surrendered
fully to the difficulty.

Becoming sick of being sick,
the doorway of surrender
becomes visible.

This is one of the
great secrets.

Verse 72

**The Solution
Becomes Obvious**

When I start believing my
knowledge is the solution,
trouble is on the way.

If I do not withhold my Love
and humanity from others, they
will not withhold theirs from me.

The sage does not exalt herself.
She exalts others, instead.

She relies on what is within,
rather than what is without.

She lets go of self-interest
and focuses on how
she can be of help.

When I stop interfering
in others' lives, trying to
relieve the noisiness
in my own life, I can see
the obvious solution within.

Verse 73

All is as It
Should Be

All of the plans
of men are feeble
when compared
with the Tao.

The Tao does not
strive or compete,
yet it excels.

The Tao does not ask,
yet it is supplied
with all it needs.

Slow, patient, calm,
relaxed, unhurried,
always at ease, yet able
to accomplish any task.

The mesh of heaven's net
is large, yet nothing
slips through.

Verse 74

The Cycle of Life

All beings are controlled by the cycle of life.
This cycle of life and death manipulates
every part of our existence, including
relationships, jobs, friendships, etc.

If we can learn to live free of the fear
of death, we can experience peace and
joy, regardless of circumstances.

How does our fear of death
influence our choices?

Do we limit our abilities by
trying to control the outcome
of our decisions?

How do we destroy others
with our actions?

Do we hold onto dead relationships or
jobs instead of being grateful, letting go,
and looking for the new birth that is coming?

Our attempts to keep alive what has died are
always fruitless and many times disastrous.

Verse 75

Stop Interfering

When we are imposed upon
to give spiritually, we starve.

This can be subtle, disguised
in obligation and duty.

First, we have to
stop interfering in
the lives of others.

Second, we can then
stop allowing others to
interfere in our lives.

We can then start allowing life
to take its course, without our
control, motivated by Love.

We begin to live free of fear,
even the fear of death.

Verse 76

Surrender to Win

All things, while alive,
are soft and pliable.
Death brings
rigidity and decay.

The same can be said for
spiritual principles.
The forceful and
unyielding are
companions of death.

Surrender and acceptance
are disciples of life.

An army that cannot change
its strategy never wins.
A tree unable to
bend will break.
A person set in their ways
will never be happy.

The narrow-minded
and defiant will fail.

The tender, yielding, and
compassionate will overcome.

Verse 77

How to Love Yourself

Love works like drawing a bow.

Where high, Love brings down.
Where low, Love lifts.

Where there is excess,
Love reduces.
When there is a deficiency,
Love replenishes.

The way of man is the opposite,
not comprehending how Love works.

Who is able to take what they have
and give to those lacking?
Only those who recognize the
unlimited power of Love.

The sage surrenders to the power of Love
to meet the needs of others, with
no desire for credit or blame.

In doing so, her self-Love
is beyond measure.

Verse 78

**Exerting
Powerlessness**

In the world, nothing is
more yielding than water.

Yet, for attacking that which
is hard and unyielding, there
is nothing better – there
is no substitute.

Use weakness to
overcome strength.

Use submissiveness to
overcome forcefulness.

In the world, no one
has this knowledge.

So the sage
exerts powerlessness
to meet any challenge,
knowing she has
unlimited strength,
not her own.

Verse 79

Love Forgives

When you reconcile a grudge,
some resentment may linger.
What can be done?

The sage takes on the
responsibility of mending.

He seeks a way to give,
a way to Love, asking
nothing in return.

The one without virtue seeks
a way to blame and deflect.

Heaven has no preference,
but always sides with
the one who forgives.

Verse 80

True Contentment

You may travel for pleasure,
knowing no location in the
world can bring lasting
inner contentment.

You may have large houses
and beautiful cars, knowing
possessions are only borrowed
and do not have real value.

You may have a successful
career and a high salary,
knowing real success
is found within.

You learn to live in the
moment, knowing freedom
from yourself is the only
source of real contentment.

This freedom is a result
of loving others through
living a surrendered life.

Verse 81

Learning to Love

Loving words are
not always beautiful.

Beautiful words are
not always loving.

Those who Love do
not need to debate.

Those who need to debate have
not yet learned how to Love.

You do not learn to
Love from a book.

You learn to
Love by loving.

The more you Love, the more
Love manifests in your life.

You start to experience
all the things you only
dreamed were possible.

Appendix A:

More About the Tao

The word "Tao" does not necessarily mean "God." Tao is better translated as "the path" – this could be any path. For example, we see many books titled "The Tao of..." on various topics. " Te" can be translated as virtue or Love. So this could be described as the "Path of Love" – or the "Path to God," especially if we think of God as being Love.

I found several Taoist philosophical ideas that support my sobriety and remind me of recovery slogans.

Nature is by design

Summer follows spring; spring follows winter – so my life is by design too.

Accepting life on life's terms

All is as it should be

My relief in life is in letting go

It's not in holding on and trying to control that I succeed.

The result was nil until we let go absolutely

Easy Does It

Being in the moment

I see no mention in the Tao Te Ching concerning the afterlife or karma, only how to live life in peace and joy, regardless of circumstances.

One day at a time

This too shall pass

There is no judgment

Similar to a mirror that reflects with no prejudice, if I learn to respond with compassion rather than self-concern and manipulation, that same Love I give is reflected back.

Your worth should never depend on another person's opinion

If you expect respect, be the first to show some

Stop thinking and end your problems

I want to understand and think through the process before I take action.

You cannot think your way into right acting;

you act your way into right thinking

Think! Think! Think! Turned upside down

What I read of Taoist philosophy helps to support the path I am already traveling. All of these ideas, and many more, perfectly fit within my recovery and Christian philosophy.

Appendix B:

The Twelve Steps of Alcoholics Anonymous

1. We admitted we were powerless over alcohol—that our lives had become unmanageable.
2. Came to believe that a Power greater than ourselves could restore us to sanity.
3. Made a decision to turn our will and our lives over to the care of God *as we understood Him*.
4. Made a searching and fearless moral inventory of ourselves.
5. Admitted to God, to ourselves, and to another human being the exact nature of our wrongs.
6. Were entirely ready to have God remove all these defects of character.
7. Humbly asked God to remove our shortcomings.
8. Made a list of all persons we had harmed, and became willing to make amends to them all.
9. Made direct amends to such people wherever possible, except when to do so would injure them or others.
10. Continued to take personal inventory and when we were wrong promptly admitted it.
11. Sought through prayer and meditation to improve our conscious contact with God *as we understood Him,* praying only for knowledge of His will for us and the power to carry that out.
12. Having had a spiritual awakening as the result of these steps, we tried to carry this message to alcoholics, and to practice these principles in all our affairs. [1] [2]

---

1. *Alcoholics Anonymous*, 4th Edition (New York: Alcoholics Anonymous World Services, Inc., 2001), 59
2. The Twelve Steps of Alcoholics Anonymous have been reprinted and adapted with the permission of Alcoholics Anonymous World Services, Inc. ("A.A.W.S."). For entire Acknowledgement, see copyright page in the front of this book.

Appendix C:

My Interpretation of the Twelve Steps

I feel inadequate writing a version of the Twelve Steps. It was suggested by writing an interpretation of the Twelve Steps, I could better demonstrate how studying the Tao Te Ching has changed how recovery works in my life. It may appear I have taken "God" out of the steps. I see a Power greater than myself in every step! I tell newcomers, "have an open mind, and your Higher Power will show up when you let go and surrender." Many thanks to Amy S., Craig M, Justin M., Scotty M., and many more for their input!

1. We admit the misery we experience by living life our way. Alcohol controls us, and we do not know what to do about it.

2. What we resist persists. We begin to see that when we stop resisting, we find strength not our own. We see this working in the lives of others, which gives us hope it will work for us.

3. We want the same relief in the rest of our lives we are beginning to discover for our alcoholism.

4. Through honest reflection, we make a list of our character traits as we perceive them in this moment. This includes not only our positive traits, but also our fears, resentments, harms done to others, and how we have been harmed — both real and imagined. We write down everything, whether we plan to share it all with someone or not.

5. By writing our 4th step list, we can admit to our innermost self some truths we may have never faced before, and we share this list with another person.

6. We begin to surrender to character traits that do not produce love in our lives.

7. We open our hearts to allow the natural changes in our lives that occur when we let love have its way.

8. We make a list of all persons we have harmed. We list them whether we are willing to make an amend or not. We ask to become willing to follow through.

9. We make direct amends to such people wherever possible, except when to do so would injure them or others.

10. When we notice selfishness, dishonesty, resentment, or fear, we choose to be open to love instead.

11. We seek to improve our conscious contact with *what is*, becoming willing to surrender more of our lives every day.

12. As we experience an ongoing spiritual awakening due to the daily practice of these steps, we carry the message of surrender to whoever appears in our path; we allow love to saturate more of our activities every day. [1]

---

1. The Twelve Steps of Alcoholics Anonymous have been reprinted and adapted with the permission of Alcoholics Anonymous World Services, Inc. ("A.A.W.S."). For entire Acknowledgement, see copyright page in the front of this book.

Appendix D:

Substituting Love for God in the Twelve Steps

1. We admitted we were powerless over alcohol—that our lives had become unmanageable.
2. Came to believe that **Love** could restore us to sanity.
3. Made a decision to turn our will and our lives over to the care of **Love** *as we understood* **Love**.
4. Made a searching and fearless moral inventory of ourselves.
5. Admitted to **Love**, to ourselves, and to another human being the exact nature of our wrongs.
6. Were entirely ready to have **Love** remove all these defects of character.
7. Humbly asked **Love** to remove our shortcomings.
8. Made a list of all persons we had harmed, and became willing to make amends to them all.
9. Made direct amends to such people wherever possible, except when to do so would injure them or others.
10. Continued to take personal inventory and when we were wrong promptly admitted it.
11. Sought through prayer and meditation to improve our conscious contact with **Love** *as we understood* **Love**, praying only for knowledge of **Love's** will for us and the power to carry that out.
12. Having had a spiritual awakening as the result of these steps, we tried to carry this message to alcoholics, and to practice these principles in all our affairs. [1]

---

1. The Twelve Steps of Alcoholics Anonymous have been reprinted and adapted with the permission of Alcoholics Anonymous World Services, Inc. ("A.A.W.S."). For entire Acknowledgement, see copyright page in the front of this book.

Appendix E:

Substituting Emptiness for God in the Twelve Steps (Taoist Version)

1. We admitted we were powerless over alcohol—that our lives had become unmanageable.
2. Came to believe that **Emptiness** could restore us to sanity.
3. Made a decision to turn our will and our lives over to the care of **Emptiness** *as we understood* **Emptiness**.
4. Made a searching and fearless moral inventory of ourselves.
5. Admitted to **Emptiness**, to ourselves, and to another human being the exact nature of our wrongs.
6. Were entirely ready to have **Emptiness** remove all these defects of character.
7. Humbly asked **Emptiness** to remove our shortcomings.
8. Made a list of all persons we had harmed, and became willing to make amends to them all.
9. Made direct amends to such people wherever possible, except when to do so would injure them or others.
10. Continued to take personal inventory and when we were wrong promptly admitted it.
11. Sought through prayer and meditation to improve our conscious contact with **Emptiness** *as we understood* **Emptiness**, praying only for knowledge of **Emptiness's** will for us and the power to carry that out.
12. Having had a spiritual awakening as the result of these steps, we tried to carry this message to alcoholics, and to practice these principles in all our affairs. [1]

---

1. The Twelve Steps of Alcoholics Anonymous have been reprinted and adapted with the permission of Alcoholics Anonymous World Services, Inc. ("A.A.W.S."). For entire Acknowledgement, see copyright page in the front of this book.

Appendix F:

Substituting Surrender for God in the Twelve Steps

1. We admitted we were powerless over alcohol—that our lives had become unmanageable.
2. Came to believe that **Surrender** could restore us to sanity.
3. Made a decision to turn our will and our lives over to the care of **Surrender** *as we understood* **Surrender**.
4. Made a searching and fearless moral inventory of ourselves.
5. Admitted to **Surrender**, to ourselves, and to another human being the exact nature of our wrongs.
6. Were entirely ready to have **Surrender** remove all these defects of character.
7. Humbly asked **Surrender** to remove our shortcomings.
8. Made a list of all persons we had harmed, and became willing to make amends to them all.
9. Made direct amends to such people wherever possible, except when to do so would injure them or others.
10. Continued to take personal inventory and when we were wrong promptly admitted it.
11. Sought through prayer and meditation to improve our conscious contact with **Surrender** *as we understood* **Surrender**, praying only for knowledge of **Surrender's** will for us and the power to carry that out.
12. Having had a spiritual awakening as the result of these steps, we tried to carry this message to alcoholics, and to practice these principles in all our affairs. [1]

---

1. The Twelve Steps of Alcoholics Anonymous have been reprinted and adapted with the permission of Alcoholics Anonymous World Services, Inc. ("A.A.W.S."). For entire Acknowledgement, see copyright page in the front of this book.

Appendix G:

Substituting Truth for God in the Twelve Steps

1. We admitted we were powerless over alcohol—that our lives had become unmanageable.
2. Came to believe that **Truth** could restore us to sanity.
3. Made a decision to turn our will and our lives over to the care of **Truth** *as we understood* **Truth**.
4. Made a searching and fearless moral inventory of ourselves.
5. Admitted to **Truth**, to ourselves, and to another human being the exact nature of our wrongs.
6. Were entirely ready to have **Truth** remove all these defects of character.
7. Humbly asked **Truth** to remove our shortcomings.
8. Made a list of all persons we had harmed, and became willing to make amends to them all.
9. Made direct amends to such people wherever possible, except when to do so would injure them or others.
10. Continued to take personal inventory and when we were wrong promptly admitted it.
11. Sought through prayer and meditation to improve our conscious contact with **Truth** *as we understood* **Truth,** praying only for knowledge of **Truth's** will for us and the power to carry that out.
12. Having had a spiritual awakening as the result of these steps, we tried to carry this message to alcoholics, and to practice these principles in all our affairs. [1]

---

1. The Twelve Steps of Alcoholics Anonymous have been reprinted and adapted with the permission of Alcoholics Anonymous World Services, Inc. ("A.A.W.S."). For entire Acknowledgement, see copyright page in the front of this book.

Appendix H:

Substituting Good for God in the Twelve Steps

1. We admitted we were powerless over alcohol—that our lives had become unmanageable.
2. Came to believe that **Good** could restore us to sanity.
3. Made a decision to turn our will and our lives over to the care of **Good** *as we understood* **Good**.
4. Made a searching and fearless moral inventory of ourselves.
5. Admitted to **Good**, to ourselves, and to another human being the exact nature of our wrongs.
6. Were entirely ready to have **Good** remove all these defects of character.
7. Humbly asked **Good** to remove our shortcomings.
8. Made a list of all persons we had harmed, and became willing to make amends to them all.
9. Made direct amends to such people wherever possible, except when to do so would injure them or others.
10. Continued to take personal inventory and when we were wrong promptly admitted it.
11. Sought through prayer and meditation to improve our conscious contact with **Good** *as we understood* **Good,** praying only for knowledge of **Good's** will for us and the power to carry that out.
12. Having had a spiritual awakening as the result of these steps, we tried to carry this message to alcoholics, and to practice these principles in all our affairs. [1]

---

1. The Twelve Steps of Alcoholics Anonymous have been reprinted and adapted with the permission of Alcoholics Anonymous World Services, Inc. ("A.A.W.S."). For entire Acknowledgement, see copyright page in the front of this book.

Appendix I:

Various Versions of the Serenity Prayer

Traditional Short Version of the Serenity Prayer

God, grant me the serenity to
accept the things I cannot change,
the courage to change the things I can,
and wisdom to know the difference.

Love Version of the Serenity Prayer

God, grant me the **Love** to
accept the things I cannot change,
the **Love** to change the things I can,
and the **Love** to know the difference.

Empty (Taoist) Version of the Serenity Prayer

God, grant me the **Emptiness**
to accept the things I cannot change,
the **Emptiness** to change the things I can,
and the **Emptiness** to know the difference.

Surrender Version of the Serenity Prayer

God, grant me the **Surrender**
to accept the things I cannot change,
the **Surrender** to change the things I can,
and the **Surrender** to know the difference.

Truth Version of the Serenity Prayer

God, grant me the **Truth** to
accept the things I cannot change,
the **Truth** to change the things I can,
and the **Truth** to know the difference.

Good Version of the Serenity Prayer

God, grant me the **Good** to
accept the things I cannot change,
the **Good** to change the things I can,
and the **Good** to know the difference.

Appendix J:

Bibliography

Stephen Mitchell, Tao Te Ching: A New English Version. New York: Harper Perennial, 1987

Jonathan Star, Tao Te Ching: The Definitive Edition (Translation and Commentary). New York: Penguin Group, 2001

Dr. Wayne W. Dyer, Change Your Thoughts Change Your Life: Living the Wisdom of the Tao. New York City: Hay House, INC., 2007

Comparative Translations side by side https://ttc.tasuki.org

Vinegar tasters - Wikipedia.

https://en.wikipedia.org/wiki/Vinegar_tasters

Index

ability, 29

abilities, 38, 74

accept, 2, 23, 24, 36, 39, 91

acceptance, 8, 10, 15, 16, 29, 76

accepting, 3, 24, 82

action(s), 6, 8, 10, 18, 20, 22 23, 30, 38, 40, 43, 63, 64, 68, 74, 82

addiction, 1, 36, 66,

admit, 85

admitted, 84, 87, 88, 89, 90, 91

alcohol, 17, 19, 84, 85, 87, 88, 89, 90, 91

alcoholic(s), 21, 84, 87, 88, 89, 90, 91

alcoholics anonymous, Preface, 84

alcoholism, Preface, 6, 62, 85

All is as it should be, Preface, 8, 73

allow(s), 10, 11, 32, 49, 57, 64

allowing, 75

already, Preface, 1, 29, 38, 47, 50, 56, 58, 82

amends, 84, 85, 87, 88, 89, 90, 91

anger, 53, 68

asset, 2

attaching, 9

attachment, 44

awareness, 49, 61

blame, 77, 79

bitterness, 63

calm, 15, 73

cautious, 15, 50

change(s), 29, 76, 85, 92, 93

channel, 28

choices, 74

choose, 3, 85

conscious contact, Preface, 84, 85, 87, 88, 89, 90, 91

content, 39, 46

contentment, 35, 44, 46, 80

control(s), 17, 29, 30, 57, 64, 74, 75, 82, 85

controlling, 46

death, 31, 33, 50, 74, 75, 76

debate, 81

decay, 8, 29, 76

defeat, 64

defect(s), 37, 84, 87, 88, 89, 90, 91

defense(s), 31, 57, 67

defiant, 76

dependence, 49

dependency, 10, 28, 39

dependent, 55

desire(s), 16, 22, 34, 57, 62, 64, 66, 77

dishonesty, 31, 69, 85

ease, 3, 15, 28, 73

effort, 7, 25, 57, 69

effortless, 38, 60

effortlessness, 42

emotions, 30

emptiness, 11, 16, 88, 93

empty, 5, 11, 22, 25, 38, 45, 92

enlightened, 33

enlightenment, 16

enough, 19, 44, 46, 54

example, 3, 8, 39, 49, 66

expectations, 9, 10, 57, 64

experience, 3, 19, 38, 43, 61, 62, 64, 65, 81, 85

extremes, 2

fail(s), 5, 6, 22, 24, 29, 39, 76

failure, 23

fear(s), 4, 16, 18, 19, 23, 26, 29, 31, 37, 38, 39, 50, 52, 53, 55, 57, 60, 62, 66, 69, 74, 75, 85

feared, 17

fearful, 56

fearless, 84, 87, 88, 89, 90, 91

feelings, 30

fight, 67

fighter, 68

fighting, 36

force, 29, 30, 38, 64

forceful, 36, 76

forcefulness, 78

forgives, 79

freedom, 37, 52, 65, 67, 80

gain, 44

gaining, 9, 42

gifts, 2, 31

give(s), 6, 7, 8, 10, 11, 34, 36, 42, 51, 61, 62, 66, 67, 75, 77, 79, 82, 85

given, 16, 24

giving, 6, 40

God, 4, 6, 16, 19, 41, 82, 84, 85, 87, 88, 89, 90, 92

Godless, 60

good, 2, 27, 35, 49, 58, 91, 93

grateful, 74

gratitude, 21, 24, 51

happiness, 58

happy, 76

harm(s), Preface, 35, 55, 85

harmed, 85, 87, 88, 89, 90, 91

harmonious, 25

harmony, 2, 4, 29, 30, 32, 55

heart(s), 18, 41, 55, 85

helping, 7, 14, 18, 23, 62

Higher Power, Preface, 5, 10, 16, 19, 20, 24, 25, 85

honest, 18

humble, 61, 66, 67

humbly, 84, 87, 88, 89, 90, 91

humility, 61

I already possess, 1, 47

illness, 71

inner voice, 12, 52

interference, 56, 64

interfering, 51, 72, 75

intuitive, 12, 52

judge, 2

judging, 58

judgment(s), 29, 82

kind, 8

kindness, 38, 63

know, 1, 4, 8, 17, 19, 21, 28, 33, 41, 43, 44, 54, 65, 71, 72, 85, 92

knowing, 15, 50, 65, 71, 78, 80

knowledge, 48, 65, 71, 72, 78, 84, 87, 88, 89, 90, 91

learn(s), 5, 6, 24, 27, 28, 36, 39, 48, 65, 74, 80, 81

learned, 20, 81

learning, 20, 52, 81

let go, Preface, 1, 9, 12, 82, 85

letting go, 57, 59, 74, 82

life, 2, 3, 4, 10, 14, 15, 16, 18, 19, 21, 22, 24, 26, 29, 30, 31, 32, 33, 34, 39, 42, 44, 50, 51, 52, 57, 58, 59, 71, 72, 74, 75, 76, 80, 81, 82, 85, 90, 93

light, 12, 16, 21, 27, 39, 52, 70

limitlessness, 35, 59

live(s), 3, 7, 8, 13, 16, 20, 21, 23, 30, 39, 49, 50, 52, 60, 66, 72, 74, 75, 80, 82, 84, 85, 87, 88, 89, 90, 91

living, 3, 7, 10, 15, 16, 18, 23, 26, 27, 29, 30, 46, 49, 50, 71, 80, 85, 93

loss, 19, 42, 44

love, 10, 16, 18, 22, 25, 31, 32, 34, 38, 39, 40, 51, 54, 55, 56, 57, 59, 60, 66, 67, 68, 72, 75, 77, 79, 81, 82, 85, 87, 92

loved, 17, 44, 66

manipulate(s), 30, 64, 74

manipulation, 10, 82

meeting(s), 18, 53

moment, 8, 20, 32, 55, 58, 80, 82, 85

need(s), 1, 7, 34, 36, 49, 73, 77, 81

needed, 15

needing, 55

Non-judgment, 2

open, 6, 8, 16, 65, 85

open-minded, 16, 85

outcome, 20, 74

outward, 12, 33, 38, 62

outwardly, 47

overcome(s), 22, 23, 36, 43, 45, 76, 78

pain, 71

paradoxical, 4, 57

past, Preface, 2, 16

path, 3, 21, 31, 41, 60, 61, 62, 63, 68, 82, 85

patient, 73

peace, 4, 16, 19, 29, 35, 38, 39, 57, 63, 74, 82

pliable, 76

possess(es), 1, 31, 36, 47, 51, 55, 64

possessed, 17

possessions, 80

Power Greater, Preface, 84, 85

powerless, 39, 84, 87, 88, 89, 90, 91

powerlessness, 13, 33, 78

prayer(s), 19, 84, 87, 88, 89, 90, 91, 92

principle(s), Preface, 4, 5, 28, 42, 43, 76, 84, 87, 88, 89, 90, 91

problem(s), 1, 9, 82

purpose, 11, 20, 39, 64, 67

ready, 41, 84, 85, 87, 88, 89, 90, 91

receive(s), 17, 27

recovery, Preface, 1, 3, 5, 28, 35, 36, 52, 62, 82, 85

reflection, 10, 85

relationship(s), 4, 8, 56, 63, 74

resentment(s), 31, 53, 69, 79, 85

resist(s), 58, 85

resistance, 30, 32, 43

resisting, 36, 85

right action, 8

satisfaction, 9

seek(s), 30, 51, 79, 85

seeking, 8, 41, 48

self, 13, 19, 22, 49, 54, 58, 63, 72, 77, 82, 85

self-love, 77

self-praise, 22

selfish, 10, 13

selfishness, 19, 31, 69

selfless action, 43

serenity, 92

service, 37

sober, Preface, 1, 2, 7, 10, 12, 19, 26, 27, 39, 41, 46

sobriety, 2, 3, 4, 5, 14, 15, 16, 17, 18, 21, 37, 41, 48, 49, 51, 54, 62, 65, 82

soft, 76

solution, 1, 19, 60, 72

spiritual awakening, 84, 85, 87, 88, 89, 90, 91

Step One, 1, 2, 4, 5, 11, 12, 13, 16, 17, 18, 19, 22, 26, 31, 32, 33, 36, 38, 39, 41, 43, 48, 50, 57, 59, 62, 69, 71, 72, 75, 76, 78

Step Two, 1, 2, 8, 9, 10, 12, 14, 15, 16, 17, 19, 29, 31, 32, 35, 39, 41, 43, 50, 52, 56, 57, 62, 65, 71, 72, 73, 76, 78

Step Three, 1, 2, 8, 9, 10, 11, 16, 19, 20, 29, 31, 32, 34, 39, 41, 50, 52, 56, 57, 58, 62, 65, 70, 71

Step Four, 1, 2, 9, 10, 16, 21, 31, 80

Step Five, 1, 2, 9, 10, 11, 16, 31, 33, 42

Step Six, 1, 2, 8, 9, 10, 16, 23, 29, 30, 31, 37, 42, 53, 57, 77

Step Seven, 1, 2, 8, 9, 10, 16, 23, 29, 30, 31, 37, 42, 53, 57, 61, 75, 77

Step Eight, 1, 4, 16, 31, 63, 79

Step Nine, 1, 4, 7, 16, 24, 29, 31, 46, 63, 68, 79

Step Ten, 1, 2, 16, 22, 30, 31, 33, 46, 53, 55, 60, 63, 69

Step Eleven, 1, 2, 5, 12, 16, 20, 24, 28, 31, 32, 35, 38, 47, 48, 55, 60, 61, 64, 66, 72, 76, 78, 81

Step Twelve, 1, 2, 3, 4, 7, 10, 13, 14, 15, 16, 23, 26, 27, 28, 31, 34, 35, 39, 43, 46, 49, 52, 54, 58, 59, 61, 62, 64, 66, 72, 77, 80, 81

step(s), Preface, 9, 16, 19, 84, 85, 87, 88, 89, 90, 91, 93

step back, 9

still, 13, 15, 16, 45, 63

stillness, 45

strength, 4, 36, 52, 55, 67, 78, 85

struggle, 8

submissive, 36

submissiveness, 78

success, 9, 23, 24, 64, 80

successful, 66, 80

suffering, Preface, 13, 35

surrender, Preface, 2, 4, 5, 10, 13, 16, 18, 22, 26, 28, 31, 33, 34, 35, 36, 37, 39, 41, 48, 51, 59, 67, 69, 70, 71, 76, 85, 89, 92

surrendered, 14, 19, 59, 71, 80

surrendering, Preface, 10, 12, 16, 19, 32, 38, 66

take(s), 2, 8, 10, 33, 34, 41, 53, 64, 66, 75, 77, 79, 82, 84, 87, 88, 89, 90, 91

taking credit, 9

Tao(ist), Preface, 16, 25, 40, 42, 68, 73, 82, 85, 88, 92, 93

task, 9, 73

teacher, 27, 43

thank you, 24

think(s), 1, 7, 25, 29, 34, 41, 65, 82

thinking, 1, 18, 71, 82

thought(s), 2, 25, 30, 93

treasure(s), 67, 69, 70

trust, 52

truth, 4, 36, 45, 57, 65, 85, 91, 93

truthful, 8

Twelve Steps, Preface, 16, 84, 85, 87, 88, 89, 90, 91

unattached, 26

unity, 42, 56

unlearn, 71

unmanageability, 38

unmanageable, 84, 87, 88, 89, 90, 91

unyielding, 36, 78

value, 2, 11, 43, 70, 80

Vinegar Tasters, Preface, 93

water, 8, 15, 32, 36, 61, 66, 78

way(s), Preface, 1, 3, 8, 14, 15, 18, 19, 21, 22, 23, 24, 25, 30, 31, 32, 37, 39, 41, 49, 50, 51, 53, 55, 57, 58, 65, 67, 68, 70, 71, 72, 76, 77, 79, 82, 85

willing, 84, 85, 87, 88, 89, 90, 91

within, 1, 8, 10, 11, 12, 21, 38, 47, 54, 70, 72, 80, 82

work(s), 5, 8, 16, 21, 27, 29, 32, 34, 36, 38, 40, 67, 68, 71, 77

yield, 22, 43

yielding, 52, 76, 78

A Place for Notes

A Place for Notes

About the Author

Buddy C. is a businessman, father, podcaster, and spiritual seeker since his early teens. Buddy made remarkable spiritual progress when he started questioning his belief systems when they did not help with his alcohol addiction. Through 12 step recovery and open-mindedness to spiritual ideas outside of his comfort zone, Buddy has been sober for over 12 years as of this writing.

Buddy C. is from Atlanta, Georgia. Buddy chairs a weekly podcast titled "The Tao of Our understanding Alcohol Recovery Podcast." Buddy sponsors men in alcohol recovery all over the world and attends online and in-person meetings regularly. With an online search, Buddy C.'s story can be found on numerous recovery podcasts. Buddy has recorded and posted over 400 contemplative recovery meditations in the free app, "Sober Meditations." He is also an active supporter of Transitions Daily.org, an online recovery group that provides daily podcasts, emails, and community support, to those in recovery worldwide.

Buddy C.'s Story

https://www.owltail.com/people/4CcB8-buddy-c/appearances

The Tao of Our Understanding Alcohol Recovery Podcast

https://taorecovery.libsyn.com/

4th Dimensioners Nightly 9 pm Eastern Online Meeting of AA.

Go to https://aa-intergroup.org/meetings and search "4th Dimensioners" or log into a free zoom account, then go to www.ZoomAAMeetings.com.

Sober Mediations

https://sobermeditations.libsyn.com/

Made in the USA
Columbia, SC
22 October 2021